Desert Life

Contents **Page**

written by Pam Holden

Red Rocket Readers™
Engineered by Flying Start Books

A desert is a big, dry place. It doesn't get much rain. It's a hard place to live because everything needs water.

We think about stuff every day. Thinking is a good thing for our minds to do.

We can get stuck in our thinking. We can worry about things that upset us. Our minds can make us think about the same stuff over and over. When we get stuck in our thinking, we can start to feel bad.

When we focus on our breathing, we can help our mind and body to get out of being stuck. Taking deep breaths can help us to relax. It can help us to stop, to slow our bodies down, and calm our thoughts.

We can take a deep breath. We can feel our chest grow big with air. We can feel the air making our belly big.

When our belly is big, we can relax and let the air out. We can feel our belly go small. We can make this breath long and slow. Our body will start to relax as we let the air out.

We can feel our thoughts slow down. We can think about how our breath feels as it moves out of our body.

It is hard to stop our minds from thinking. We can tell our thoughts to wait. We can choose to focus on our breath coming and going.

focus on our breath

When you feel stuck, you can belly breathe. You can do it when you are sad. You can do it to feel calm.

When we feel like we need to calm our minds, we can use our belly breathing to help us.

working on our breathing

We can do it anywhere – in the classroom, playing on the playground, and at home.

Living in a desert is a hard life for plants, animals, and people.

sandstorm